Citizen Guides

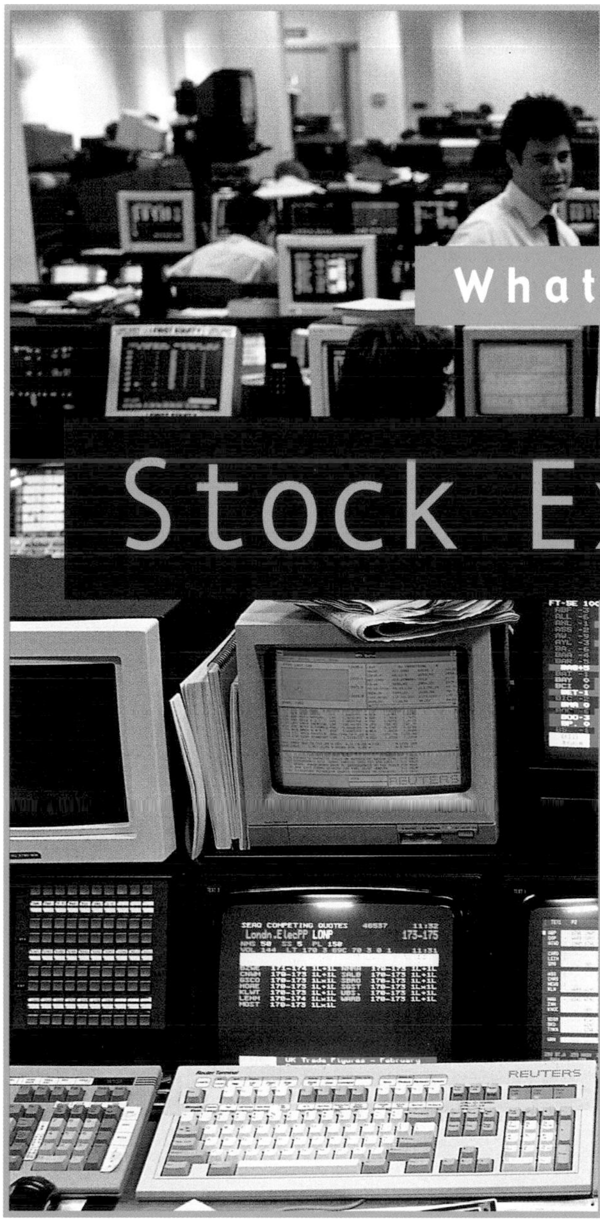

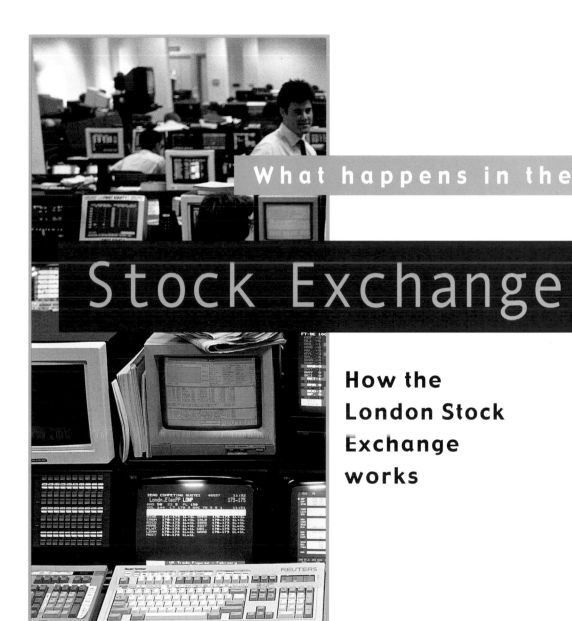

What happens in the

Stock Exchange

How the London Stock Exchange works

Soraya Moeng

W
FRANKLIN WATTS
LONDON • SYDNEY

About the author

Soraya Moeng studied English at King's College, London and University College, London. She has worked as an editor and journalist for organisations such as ITN, the *Financial Times* Group and the London Stock Exchange.

Key words

To help you find your way around this book, key words are printed in **bold**. You can find some of these words in the glossary on pages 30-31.

Illustrations Alastair Taylor/The Inkshed

Designer Magda Weldon
Art Director Jonathan Hair
Editor Penny Clarke
Editor-in-Chief John C. Miles

First published in 2000
by Franklin Watts
96 Leonard Street
London
EC2A 4XD

Franklin Watts Australia
56 O'Riordan Street
Alexandria
NSW 2015

ISBN 0 7496 3763 3

Dewey classification: 332.63

A CIP catalogue record
for this book is available
from the British Library.

Printed in Malaysia

Contents

Introduction

The London Stock Exchange is the UK's principal stock market. Here, companies raise money in order to expand their businesses, and investors buy and sell shares hoping to make a profit.

Companies on the Exchange

Many household names in Britain are listed on the **London Stock Exchange**, but in fact the companies **quoted** on its **markets** come from more than 60 countries around the world.

The companies represented on the Exchange range from supermarkets to banks and from utility companies to football clubs. What we ourselves buy and use can influence the performance of a company and its shares on the Stock Exchange.

Many people in the United Kingdom are affected by what happens in the Stock Exchange through their

THE LONDON STOCK EXCHANGE is situated in the City of London. This view from the Exchange Tower shows some famous landmarks, including the dome of St Paul's Cathedral, centre right.

THE LOGO of the London Stock Exchange incorporates the coat of arms of the City of London.

investments. More than 12.5 million people now own **shares** (also called **securities**), either by direct buying or through the receipt of **windfall shares** – for example, when a building society becomes a bank and awards shares to its members. Share owners are known as **shareholders** and each of them owns a part of that **Public Limited Company**, or **plc**.

Many people invest for their future by starting a **pension scheme** or taking out a **life assurance policy**. These people are also affected by the progress of the stock market. The companies which run these plans are likely to have invested part of their funds in companies on the Exchange.

The Exchange and the City

The London Stock Exchange is one of the most important financial institutions in the **City of London**, where the Bank of England and the headquarters of many national and foreign banks are located. Other exchanges, such as the London Metal Exchange, the Baltic Exchange and the London International Financial Futures and Options Exchange (LIFFE) are also situated in the part of the **City** known as 'the Square Mile'. Together, they help to make London one of the leading financial centres in the world.

Early history

To understand fully what the London Stock Exchange does, and how it came to occupy its position in the City, it is important to know a little of its long and interesting history.

In the late 1600s, the first laws were introduced to control the market where people met to buy and sell shares.

Joint-stock companies

The origins of the London Stock Exchange stretch back to the middle of the 16th century, when **merchant venturers** wanted to explore and trade in the Far East. It cost a lot of money to equip these expeditions, so to raise the money necessary, **joint-stock** companies were set up. The first one was the **Muscovy Company**, founded in 1553.

The merchants shared the risk of the project by buying a stake, or **share**, in the company. They could make a big **profit** if the expedition was successful. Members of the public could also buy shares. Together, all the shareholders contributed **capital** for the project; the company was run by an elected **governor** and deputies.

Coffee houses and brokers

Towards the end of the 17th century trade had increased rapidly, and the market for shares in joint-stock companies had expanded. Shares were bought and sold face-to-face by brokers – a system known as 'open outcry'.

The brokers at that time were men who traded in the commodities of the companies of the day. Notoriously noisy and rowdy, they had already been banned from the Royal Exchange building,

THIS PRINT of the late 1700s shows rowdy brokers meeting at a coffee house.

where deals were agreed. They began moving to the coffee houses in nearby Change Alley, where they could conduct their business in greater comfort. Chief among these establishments was one known as Jonathan's.

A subscription club at Jonathan's was set up in the late 1760s by 150 brokers – members were charged six pence a day as an entry fee. When the old clubroom was destroyed by fire, a new subscription room called 'New Jonathan's' was opened in Threadneedle Street. In 1773 its members voted to change the name to the Stock Exchange.

By the end of the 18th century the Stock Exchange needed new premises, and the foundation stone of the new building was laid in 1801. The present Exchange building occupies the same site.

Industrial revolution

The Victorian era saw rapid industrialisation and major advances in transport and technology. Developing railways and canals and expanding production of coal and steel needed money. Much of this capital was raised by people buying shares on the Stock Exchange.

The 20th century and beyond

Following World War I (1914-18), the 1920s were successful years for stock markets worldwide. However, in 1929, the "Crash" on Wall Street (the principal US Stock Exchange) marked the end of this prosperity.

BROOKLYN DAILY EAGLE

And Complete Long Island News

LATE NEWS — WALL STREET 1:15 PRICES ★★

89th YEAR—No. 295. ★ NEW YORK CITY, THURSDAY, OCTOBER 24, 1929. ★ 32 PAGES THREE CENTS

WALL ST. IN PANIC AS STOCKS CRASH

Attempt Made to Kill Italy's Crown Prince

ASSASSIN CAUGHT IN BRUSSELS MOB; PRINCE UNHURT

Royal Suitor Was About to Lay Wreath on Unknown Soldiers' Tomb.

Princess, Deeply Moved, Falls Into Fiance's Arms and Kisses Him

Hollywood Fire Destroys Films Worth Millions

Consolidated Studios Are Swept by Flames Fatal to One—Master Pictures Burned Include Many New Talkie Productions.

ATTEMPT MADE ON LIFE

Crown Prince Humbert.

FEAR 52 PERISHED IN LAKE MICHIGAN; FERRY IS MISSING

Wreckage Picked Up Indicates Craft Went Down With All Aboard.

PIECE OF PLANE LIKE DITEMAN'S IS FOUND AT SEA

Black and Orange Wreckage Indicates Daring Flier Went to Death.

High Duty Group Gave $700,000 to Coolidge Drive

Grundy Agrees Rates Went Up Due to His Activities as Propagandist. Favors More Lobbying to 'Carry Out Voters' Wish.'

FOR MORE LOBBYISTS

JOSEPH R. GRUNDY

STOCKS CRASH IN RUSH TO SELL; BILLIONS LOST

Morgan, Mitchell Buying Stocks in Effort to Check Rush to Unload.

CARNEGIE CHARGE OF PAID ATHLETES ROUSES COLLEGES

Survey Finds Shopping for Stars Is General. Remedies Now in Force.

HOOVER'S TRAIN HALTED BY AUTO PLACED ON RAILS

2 Negroes Admit Scheme to Collect Insurance for Loss of Machine.

WARDER SOUGHT TO KEEP SEA TRIP SECRET, AID SAYS

Woman Testifies She Was Asked to Say Nothing About Plans.

SOMERS NAMED AS HEAD OF NEW EXCHANGE BANK

Damman Is Chosen for Chairman of Board. Miller Vice President.

10 ARABS SENTENCED TO LIFE TERMS FOR PALESTINE MASSACRE

Today's News

DANCERS IN PANIC AS MAN IS STABBED; POLICE SEIZE 5 MEN

Mae Murray Suit Asks $250,000 for Foot Hurt

DOG TALKIE STAR KEEPS SILENCE IN AUTO STORE WRECK

Two Are Held in Bail As Speakeasy Owners

THE EAGLE INDEX

SHARE PRICES CRASHED in 1929, causing panic.

Post-war changes

War broke out again in 1939, and the City of London endured days and nights of bombing during World War II (1939-45). In the 1950s the Labour government brought many industries, such as gas, electricity, coal and railways into **public ownership**. More than £3,500 million of **government stock** was issued so the government could buy out **private shareholders**

A new home

Through the 1960s industry boomed, and London needed a larger and more modern stock exchange. A new building was opened by the Queen in 1972, while a customised **trading floor** in the basement began operation in 1973. And for the first time, women were admitted.

In the early 1980s the government also wanted to open up the **financial services industry** to more competition. This led to the changes known as the **Big Bang**.

A VIEW OF THE Stock Exchange Tower in the City of London. The building in front is the Bank of England.

New ownership rules and the abolition of minimum **commission** for **share trading** – to encourage **smaller investors** – were two of the changes. The third was to allow **brokers/dealers** to both represent clients in the market and buy and sell shares on behalf of their firms.

In 1986, the buying and selling of shares began electronically, replacing the face-to-face system that had been in use for more than 200 years.

Into the 21st century

The 1990s saw important changes to the way in which the world's financial markets operate. The **Internet** in particular is important, and there are now several **electronic exchanges**, or **ECN**s, operating internationally.

Most recently, the London Stock Exchange itself became a Public Limited Company. Shares in the Exchange will be traded and owned by shareholders.

A high-tech industry

Also important in the 2000s is how technology affects the financial world. The information from London's markets is now transmitted electronically to over 90,000 computer screens around the world.

Trading has come a long way since the days of the stockjobbers conducting face-to-face deals in Jonathan's Coffee House. However, the underlying principle of the Exchange remains unchanged – it is still a marketplace for companies to raise money and for people to buy and sell shares.

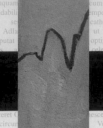

What the Stock Exchange does

Knowing something about the history of the Stock Exchange, it is easier to understand why it has been important to the development of the UK's economy. Today, the Exchange performs three main functions.

Company services

The London Stock Exchange provides several different **markets** where shares are traded. Companies join up to raise money and have their shares traded publicly. The markets that the Exchange provides are supported by a range of services such as the **Regulatory News Service (RNS)** system. This service ensures that **company announcements** are accurate and communicated promptly. This is particularly important for company news that might have an impact on the price of any share listed on the Exchange.

Trading services

Sophisticated **computer services** are operated by the Exchange to allow efficient trading of companies' shares. The Exchange is also

THE THREE MAIN SERVICES provided by the London Stock Exchange.

SHARE AWARE 1999
Performance of £100 invested in UK
companies compared with UK
GET YOUR SHARE OF GREAT BRITISH COMPANIES
Get Share Aware
London STOCK EXCHANGE
1989
1990
1991
1992
1993
1994
1998
10 YEARS

SHARE AWARE aims to encourage ordinary people to invest in shares. Well-known TV personalities make presentations on the benefits of share ownership.

a **Recognised Investment Exchange**. This means that it is responsible for the orderly operation and **regulation** of its markets.

Information services

This function brings **real-time** (up to the minute) **share price information** to computer screens around the world, enabling people to keep abreast of what is going on in London's financial markets.

You can keep track of share prices through **newspapers**, the **Internet** and **television**. Shares are indexed using **FTSE** classifications. The most well-known classification is the **FTSE 100** or **'Footsie'**, which you see and hear quoted in many news items about the Stock Exchange.

The Exchange also promotes the benefits of **share ownership** among the general public through its **Share Aware** programme.

Types of shares

There are many types of investments traded on the London Stock Exchange. There are ordinary shares, or equities, bonds and specialist securities. For all of these, there are computerised dealing systems.

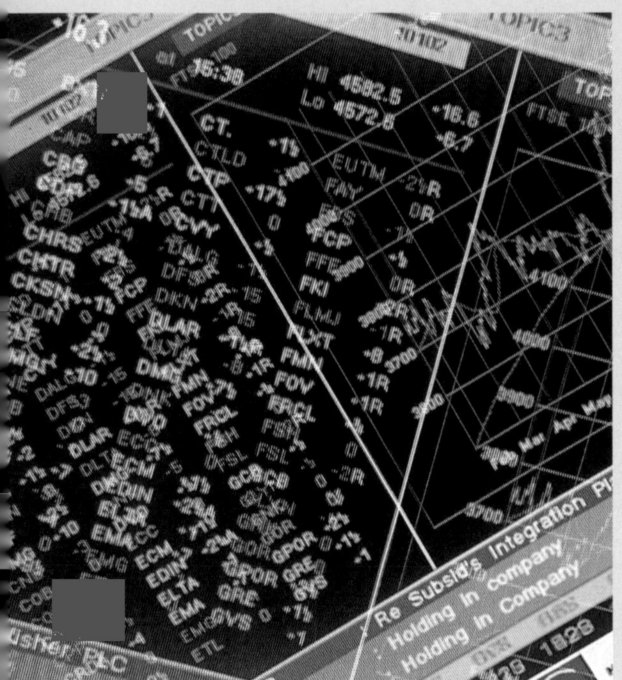

TRADING on the London Stock Exchange creates a blur of buying and selling prices on dealers' screens.

Ordinary shares

These are the shares issued by companies to raise money through selling the shares to the general public. They are also known as **UK equities.** Companies outside the UK also issue shares, known as **overseas equities.**

Bonds

Bonds are **securities** issued by the government in order to raise money to fund its spending. They are also known as **gilts** or **gilt-edged securities** and give the owner a regular payment, called an **interest payment**, every year. The issuer also guarantees a **redemption date**, which means that a set amount of money will be repaid at a fixed date in the future. **Companies** can also issue bonds. These are known as **fixed interest securities.** Like gilts, they provide the owner with a regular interest payment and a final lump sum.

Specialist securities

Other kinds of investments traded on the London Stock Exchange include **eurobonds**, **warrants** and **depositary receipts.** These kinds of securities are likely to be bought by experienced investors and not by the small investor.

AS AN INVESTOR, you can channel your money into a wide variety of securities.

Trading securities

The London Stock Exchange operates two markets – the **main market**, where you can find many UK and international companies, and **AIM**, the Exchange's market for fledgling and growing companies.

Within the main market there is also **techMARK**. This is a market that groups together specialist **high-tech** companies from many different areas.

After listing

Once a company is **listed** on one of the Exchange's markets and has raised money through a **share issue**, it can raise more money if necessary by issuing further shares. Further share issues not only raise capital; they also ensure that the company's profile is kept high among investors.

Trading shares

Sophisticated computerised systems at the London Stock Exchange allow securities to be traded smoothly and quickly.

In 1997 the Exchange introduced **SETS**, which is also known as the **electronic order book**. This system is the trading service for the **FTSE (Footsie) 100** – the top 100 companies on the Exchange – and other large companies. Brokers enter **'buy'** and **'sell' orders** into the system and the computer automatically matches up those wanting to sell shares with those wanting to buy.

Other important trading services are called **SEAQ** and **SEATS PLUS** (see glossary).

Floating a company

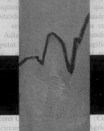

Companies float, or list, on the Stock Exchange for two main reasons. The first is to raise money. The second is to make shares available to a wide range of investors and raise the company's overall profile.

Liquidity and profile

The ease with which a company's shares can be traded is known as its **liquidity** – the better the liquidity, the easier it is to raise money.

More visible to the general public is the higher profile which **floating**, or **listing**, on the stock market can bring to a company. Being listed on a stock market can help to reassure a company's **customers** and **clients** and provide it with a useful introduction in other countries if the directors are looking to expand overseas.

Companies do not have to list on just one exchange – many large businesses are listed on more than one around the world. This increases their visibility and profile.

Before the float

If the directors of a company decide to float it on the stock market they need to appoint advisers, such as **accountants**, **lawyers** and **stockbrokers**, to help them through the **listing process**.

The process has to be carefully planned by the directors. They issue a **prospectus** (a document saying why people should invest in the company), market and advertise the **share issue** and meet potential investors.

DIRECTORS OF COMPANIES listing on the London Stock Exchange attend a special ceremony. Here the Chairman of the Exchange welcomes executives of a Chinese company.

The float

Once listed, a public company has to be **transparent to the market** in order to keep trading fair for all. Obligations range from the punctual publication of a company's **annual report** to ensuring that **price-sensitive information** – which might affect the daily share price – is made available to all investors at the same time. If a company breaks the rules it can be **suspended from trading** while an investigation is conducted.

In spite of the benefits of flotation, some companies decide to remain private. A flotation comes with strict **rules** and **responsibilities**. These include being subject to the conditions of the market at any given time – share prices can go down as well as up.

The **performance** of a listed company falls under much closer scrutiny. This can be good when the company's shares are performing well, but much less welcome if they under-perform.

How a company floats

A company can choose three different ways in which to come to the stock market: offer for sale, placing or introduction. Each option has different benefits for the company.

Offer for sale

This is when a company's **sponsor** offers the shares to **private** and/or **institutional investors** – usually at a **fixed price** per share.

Offer for sale is the preferred method for a company which is looking to raise substantial amounts of capital for its business. An offer for sale will be advertised in the national press.

Placing

This is a more specific way of raising capital. Here the company raising money offers its shares to a selected number of **institutional investors**. This allows the company to choose its investors. **Placing** is the most popular option for companies coming to the stock market for the first time.

Introduction

An **introduction** is when a company joins the market without raising capital. It can opt for this method if more than 25 per cent of its shares are in **public hands**.

Although straightforward, an introduction does not give a company the same high profile as other ways of flotation.

Britain's top 100 companies are listed in the FTSE (Footsie) 100 index.

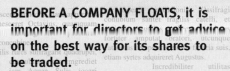

BEFORE A COMPANY FLOATS, it is important for directors to get advice on the best way for its shares to be traded.

How shares are traded

Once a company has successfully listed on the stock market its shares are bought and sold by **market makers** – large firms that buy and sell **shares** during the **trading hours** of the Exchange.

The price at which a market maker will buy shares is known as a **bid**. The price at which it will sell is known as an **offer**.

Stockbroking firms (which may be working for themselves or on behalf of clients) contact market makers by telephone or computer to buy or sell shares. They do this when they feel the prices the market makers quote for shares best meet their (or their clients') requirements. Market makers constantly change their quotes for the buy and sell prices of shares.

Changes in share prices are influenced by many factors. These include the strength of demand for a company's shares and by other news, for example company mergers and acquisitions.

Prices and the electronic order book

For the largest companies a different trading system is used. The **FTSE 100** companies and a number of **FTSE 250** ones – the largest businesses on the stock market – are traded using the electronic service called **SETS**. Also known as the **order book**, SETS matches up 'buy' and 'sell' orders and puts the orders in hand automatically.

Investing in stocks and shares 1

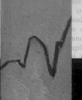

Just as there are considerable benefits for a company coming to the public market, there are many advantages for someone who wishes to invest in the shares of the companies listed on the Exchange.

Ordinary shares

When you become a **shareholder** in a company, you own a stake in it. For the private investor the most common kind of share is known as the **ordinary share**. This kind of share gives you a part of any **profits** the company may make, and the right to **vote** at a company's **annual meeting**.

Dividends

A shareholder is rewarded for investing in a company in the form of **dividends** which are usually paid twice a year. Owners of ordinary shares will receive **variable dividends.** Another kind of share is a **preference share** where the holders receive a **fixed dividend**.

Companies performing well may increase dividends each year, but companies that are performing badly might only be able to pay a small dividend – or sometimes nothing at all. If a company does very badly and is forced to **wind up**, the shareholders might be entitled to a share of the money made by selling off the company's **assets**.

Capital growth

Owning shares can be a beneficial way to save. One of the ways in which shares are different from

SHARE PRICES may rise, making you a profit on your initial investment (top). However, they can also fall, making you a loss (bottom).

putting your money into a savings account is the possibility of **capital growth**.

A company's **share price** changes in value all the time – the value of your shares can go down as well as up. If the company in which you have invested performs well, the shares may increase in value (capital growth) and you may be able to sell your shares for more than you paid for them.

Investing in shares can be a good way to make money over a long period of time. However, there is an element of risk involved in investing in the stock market, as the value of your shares may well go down. If this happens then you may make a loss.

Two ways to invest

There are two main ways in which you can invest in the stock market:

Direct investment – in this method, you make your own decision about which shares to buy, or get help from an adviser. You can buy shares in one company or a range of companies. Buying shares in a range of companies helps reduce **risk** and allows you to build up a **portfolio** of shares.

Indirect investment – this method includes schemes such as **investment trusts** and **unit trusts**. **Fund managers** decide which shares to invest in. This method also lessens the investment's risk .

Investing in stocks and shares 2

Provided people are realistic and responsible with the money they want to put into the stock market, investing in shares can be a simple and fascinating way in which to see money grow.

Investment clubs

One way of investing which is becoming increasingly popular in the UK is to be part of an **investment club**. This is where a group of people each put in some money and have informal meetings to decide which companies to invest in. It is much easier to understand and access the stock market now, as books, magazines and the Internet have helped to raise people's awareness of the benefits of stock market investment.

MANY PEOPLE rely on a financial expert to advise them on which shares to invest their money in.

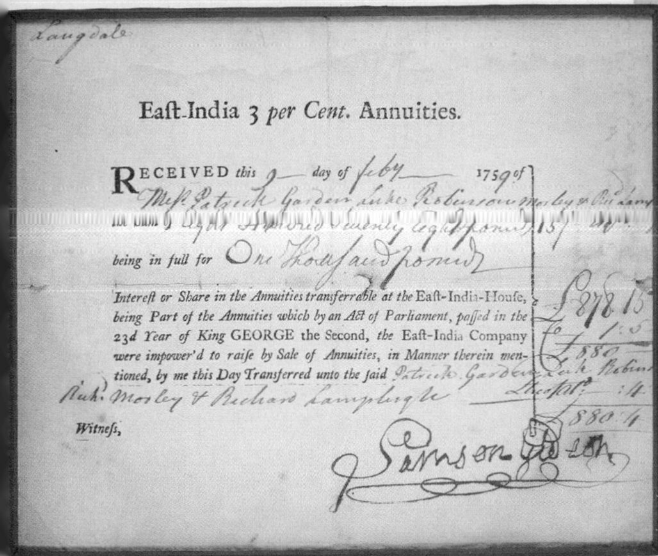
East-India 3 *per Cent.* Annuities.

RECEIVED *this* 9 *day of* Feby 1759

being in full for One Thousand pound

Interest or Share in the Annuities transferrable at the East-India-House, *being Part of the Annuities which by an Act of Parliament, passed in the* 23*d Year of King* GEORGE *the* Second, *the* East-India Company *were impower'd to raise by Sale of Annuities, in Manner therein mentioned, by me this Day Transferred unto the said*

Witness,

IN THE PAST, when you bought shares you were issued with a paper certificate, such as this one from the 1700s. Today, many share records are held on computer.

How investors buy and sell shares

There are three main ways in which investors can buy and sell shares:

Execution-only – this is when you contact your **stockbroker** or **bank** with instructions to buy or sell shares. The broker cannot give you advice and will not comment on your decisions.

Advisory service – this time the bank or stockbroker **advises** you which shares are good ones to buy or sell. They may also contact you with any further suggestions about your shares.

Discretionary service – here you give your bank or stockbroker permission to buy and sell shares on your behalf. They handle all the administration involved in agreeing and confirming the deal.

One other way of share dealing is to use the Internet or **on-line dealing,** which can make the process much quicker and easier.

Once you have bought shares

Once you have bought your shares, the **share certificate** – proof of share ownership – can be held as an **electronic record** or as a **paper certificate.** In the UK, all share transactions go through a settlement system called **CREST**. This computerised system handles all the **completion-of-deal arrangements** once you have agreed to buy or sell shares.

In addition to small investors, most companies have institutional investors. These are firms such as pension or insurance companies that invest in shares on a large scale. They help give companies larger amounts of money to allow them to expand.

Keeping an eye on the markets

There are many ways in which investors can keep track of share prices and get other information about their money. Indicators of how shares are performing are called indices (singular index).

Keeping track

Once you have bought some shares it is possible to keep track of the progress of the company in a number of ways.

Most national newspapers carry **daily share prices**. They also have business pages with articles about companies in the news. Specialist investment magazines have in-depth articles.

The Internet is a good source of information, and there are several companies that offer both on-line dealing and information services. Many companies have websites, which contain useful information for investors.

Television services such as Ceefax and Teletext are a very useful and accessible way for people to monitor the progress of their shares.

How to read share prices

The **stock market section** in a newspaper or on television can look daunting, but the columns of figures are simply a detailed record of what took place on the stock market on the previous business day. Simple calculations tell you how a particular company performed. To make it easier for investors to see how their shares are doing, companies are

THE STOCK MARKET PAGES can appear confusing, but they are easier to read when you know what you're actually looking at.

listed alphabetically by **sector**, such as General Retailers, Pharmaceuticals and Leisure, Entertainment & Hotels. This makes it much easier for investors to compare a company's performance with others in the same group.

Here is an entry in the stock market listings for an imaginary book publisher:

Media & Photography – ABC Books

Price (p)	**High** (p)	**Low** (p)	**+/-** (p)	**Yield** (%)	**P/E**
195	250	180	+3	5	70

ABC Books is the **name** of the company.

The **price** is the mid-point of the prices at which you could have bought or sold shares at the close of business yesterday (usually quoted in pence).

The **high** is the highest price ABC's shares have reached so far this year.

The **low** is the lowest price ABC's shares have reached so far this year.

The **+/-** figure shows whether the shares closed up or down on the previous day's trading. In this example, ABC Books closed up 3 pence on the previous day's figure.

The **yield** is the annual return on your money. It is based on the latest dividends from the company. It is expressed as a percentage of the current price of the shares.

The **P/E** or **Price/Earnings Ratio** is the current share price divided by the annual earnings per share. It is a measure of the level of confidence investors have in a company. ABC's current P/E is high, suggesting that confidence in the company is high.

Regulating the ups and downs

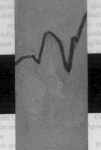

It is important that the Stock Exchange is properly regulated to maintain the confidence of investors and to make sure that people want to continue to invest their money in shares.

The FSA

Millions of people in the UK are shareholders or own stocks through firms which invest in the stock market. They are protected by strict laws put in place by the Treasury which are enforced by the **Financial Services Authority (FSA)**.

Continuous regulation

Stockbroking firms, market makers and trading in companies are regulated continuously to ensure they are not breaking any of the rules of conduct.

An example of this might be so-called **'insider dealing'** where a person manages to obtain secret information about a company – perhaps a **merger** with another company – that will raise its share price. The person buys a lot of shares at the old low price and sells when the share price shoots up, making a lot of money on the transaction.

Company information should be communicated to everyone at the same time in a transparent way, making investment fair.

Regulation of this sort of activity helps to reassure investors, both private and institutional, that the stock market is a good place to invest.

A bull or a bear?

Although there are many limits in place to minimise the risk for investors, it is difficult to predict how a stock market will perform from one day to the next. If the market is doing well it is known as a **bull market**. Investors who buy a security in the hope of selling it at a higher price are known as **bulls**.

Conversely, if the market is falling it is known as a **bear market**, and investors who sell their securities with a view to buying them back at a lower price are known as **bears**.

The London Stock Exchange's markets include companies from all sectors and of all sizes which help to drive the country's financial progress. By owning shares, an individual can help companies to grow and be a part of that drive – while saving for his or her long-term future.

'BULLS' PROSPER when share prices are on the rise and market confidence is high (left). 'Bears' prosper when both share prices and confidence fall (right).

Stock exchanges around the world

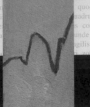

Many countries have stock exchanges which act, as in the UK, as a market place for companies to raise money. Here is a quick round-up of major stock exchanges around the world.

USA

The US has two stock exchanges – the **New York Stock Exchange (NYSE)** situated on **Wall Street,** and the **National Association of Securities Dealers Automated Quotation system (NASDAQ).** The origins of the NYSE stretch back to 1792. Its index is known as the Dow Jones. Nasdaq was set up in 1971.

Japan

Tokyo's stock exchange was set up in 1878. Its main index is known as the **Nikkei**.

Hong Kong

The Hong Kong Stock Exchange's index is called the **Hang Seng**.

Germany

Based in Frankfurt, Germany's stock exchange is the **Deutsche Börse**. Frankfurt is also the home of the **European Central Bank (ECB)**.

In May 2000 the London Stock Exchange and Deutsche Börse announced plans to merge and create the largest European stock market.

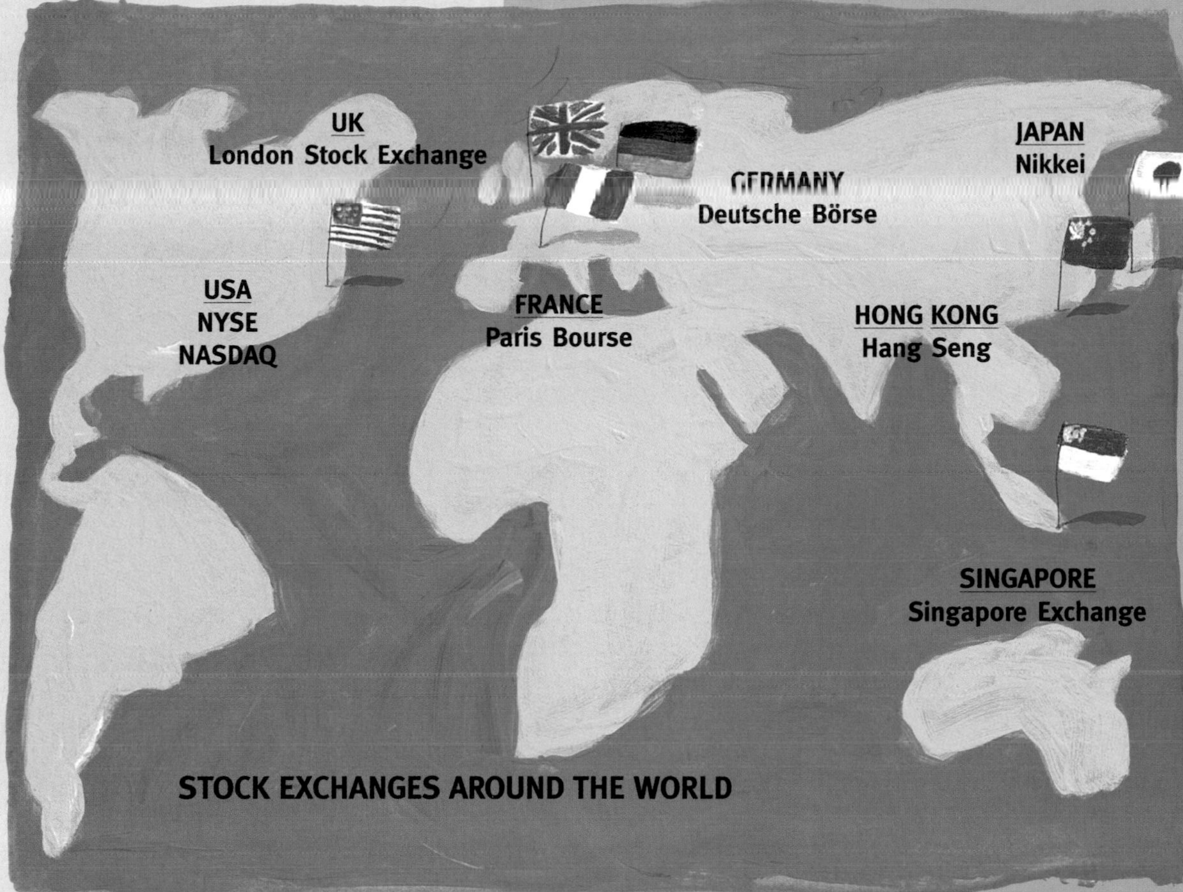

France

Paris Bourse is the name of the French national stock exchange.

Singapore

The **Singapore Exchange** was created in 1999 after the two national stock exchanges, SIMEX and SES, merged.

EASDAQ

The **European Association of Securities Dealers Automated Quotation exchange (EASDAQ)** is modelled on the US Nasdaq market. It trades shares from across Europe.

Glossary

AIM The Exchange's market for fledgling companies. The initials stand for Alternative Investment Market.

Bear An investor who has sold a security in the hope of buying it back at a lower price.

Bear market A market in which bears would prosper – a falling market.

Bid The price at which a market maker will buy shares.

Broker A firm which provides advice and dealing services to the public, and which can deal on its own account.

Bull An investor who has bought a security in the hope of selling it at a higher price.

Bull market A market in which bulls would prosper – a rising market.

Capital Another term for money or funds.

Commission The fee a broker charges for transactions.

CREST The UK's share settlement system, through which deals made on the Exchange's markets can be settled.

Dividend A shareholder's share of any company profits – usually paid twice a year.

Financial Services Authority (FSA) The agency appointed by the UK government to oversee the regulation of the investment industry.

Flotation When a company's shares start trading on the Stock Exchange.

FTSE and FTSE indices A company owned by the *Financial Times* newspaper (FT) and the London Stock Exchange (SE), which is responsible for the indices covering large, medium and small companies and showing the trend of price movements.

FTSE 100 (Footsie) The popular name for the FTSE 100 index of the UK's largest 100 companies by market capitalisation.

Insider dealing The purchase or sale of securities by someone who possesses 'inside' information not yet available to the market. In the UK such deals are a criminal offence.

Investment trusts Companies quoted on the stock market whose business is managing a portfolio of shares in other companies.

Liquidity The ease with which a security can be traded on the market. It refers to the amount of trading in a company's shares.

Market makers Firms which are obliged to offer to buy and sell securities in which they are registered during official trading hours.

Nominees Companies that hold shares electronically on behalf of shareholders.

Offer The price at which a market maker will sell shares.

Ordinary share The most common form of share. Holders may receive dividends in line with the company's profitability.

Portfolio Shares held in a range of companies.

Preference share These are normally fixed-income shares whose holders have the right to receive dividends before ordinary shareholders.

Public Limited Company (plc) A company whose shares may be purchased by the public.

Rights issues An invitation to existing shareholders to purchase additional shares in the company.

SEAQ The Stock Exchange Automated Quotations system for UK securities. It is a continuously updated computer database containing price quotations and trade reports.

SEAQ International The Stock Exchange Automated Quotations system for international equities.

Security or securities The general name for stocks and shares of all types.

SETS The Stock Exchange Electronic Trading System, otherwise known as the 'order book'.

SEATS PLUS A system that supports both market maker quotes and an order book.

Settlement The process of transferring stock from seller to buyer and arranging the corresponding money transfer. See CREST.

Share certificate A paper copy of the certificate which proves an investor owns shares in a company.

techMARK Set up in November 1999, this market groups together technology companies from across the main market.

Unit trusts Funds, made up of many investors' contributions, divided into equal units – like investment trusts they also invest in stock markets worldwide. The decisions on where to invest the funds are made by the managers of the unit trusts.

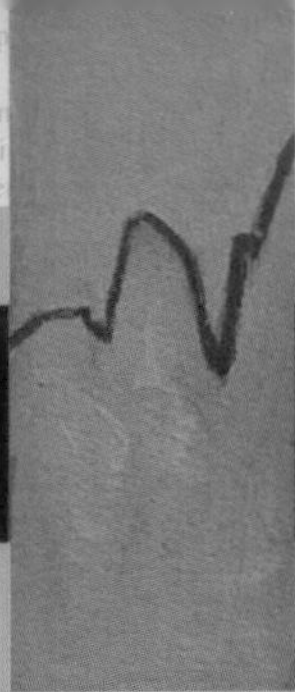

Index

PICTURE CREDITS
Cover image: London Stock Exchange plc
Guildhall Art Gallery, Corporation of London p. 9 (*Stockjobbers Extraordinary* by Robert Dighton, c. 1795)
Image Bank p. 22
London Stock Exchange plc pp. 1, 3, 5, 6, 7, 11, 13, 14, 17, 19, 23
Mary Evans Picture Library p. 10